A Night Ou

CW00828190

A Comedy

Frank Vickery

Samuel French – London
New York – Sydney – Toronto – Hollywood

A NIGHT OUT

First performed at the Berwyn Theatre, Nant-Y-Moel on
the 25th March, 1981, and subsequently at the Sherman
Theatre, Cardiff, with the following cast of characters:

Doreen	Suzanne Hughes
Dad	Garfield Longden
Mam	Lilian Davies
Eric	Martyn Wake

Directed by Ann Lewis
Designed by Garfield Longden

The action of the play takes place in the living-room of
the family's suburban house

Time—the present

To Suzanne

A NIGHT OUT*

A living-room

Part of the hall can be seen back C *stage with stairs leading* L *to the bedrooms and a passageway* R *to the front door and street. On the bottom of the banisters are a jacket and raincoat. Just in front of the stairs is a doorway which leads to the kitchen. There is no door but there are plastic streamers hanging from the architrave. The room can only be described as a tip. On stage there is a dining-table, complete with dirty tea dishes, a box of groceries and the remains of a Chinese meal. There is a dining-chair, an armchair, with a fur coat slung over the back, a settee, a sideboard, a television, a coffee-table with a record player and records on it and a hall stand with coats and umbrellas. The whole impression of the room is one of physical chaos. Every drawer is packed with articles, every surface covered with junk. Magazines and papers are stuffed under cushions, shoes etc. are under the tables. There is a mirror on the wall between the dining-table and the television and there are letters and bills hanging from behind it. The sideboard is the most cluttered piece of furniture, anything can be placed on it although there are some essential articles which must be included such as a clock, a telephone, a purse, a vase and a mirror. There is an electric socket on the wall left of the kitchen doorway and a calendar on the wall right of the kitchen doorway. There is a pigeon basket left of the sideboard*

As the CURTAIN *rises there is no-one on stage*

After a few seconds Doreen descends the stairs on tip toe. She is a girl in her late teens who would not, under any circumstances, be considered a beauty. She is frumpy, wears flat shoes and a cardigan over a flowered dress. She has a centre parting. As the room is empty she takes the opportunity to make a private phone call. After moving several articles on the sideboard, she finds the phone and dials

---

*N.B. Paragraph 3 on page ii of this Acting Edition regarding photocopying and video-recording should be carefully read.

Doreen (*sotto voce*) Hello lollipop? . . . Of course it's me, who else
calls you lollipop? . . . I can't speak up. . . . No I can't. Look,
everything's all right. They're going out. . . . Yes, they're getting
ready now. . . . About twenty minutes. . . . Okay then. . . . I'll be
waiting (*She giggles*) I've made the bed, (*louder*) I said I've made
the . . . in about twenty minutes then, all right? Bye, bye sugar. I
love you, my little saccharin. (*She hangs up immediately*)

Dad enters down the stairs holding up two ties

Dad Which one did you . . . ? (*He looks around the room; exaspera-
tedly to Doreen*) Where the hell has your mother gone now?
Doreen She's just popped out to the shop.
Dad (*shouting*) To the where?
Doreen She laddered her tights. She's gone to get a new pair.
Dad Are you any good with ties?
Doreen (*beginning to tidy up the settee*) It's left over right.
Dad (*turning towards her*) I know how to do the bloody thing up. I
mean choice. What colour? (*He holds them up towards her*)
Doreen (*looking over her shoulder as she stuffs a magazine under a
cushion*) The blue one.
Dad (*shaking his head*) I rather fancied the mauve myself.
Doreen That's why you always ask advice.
Dad The blue one then. (*He puts the mauve tie down on the
television, then puts on the blue one in front of the mirror*)
Doreen Unless you want to go fancy dress.
Dad What are you still doing here anyway? I thought you were
going out tonight.

Doreen freezes momentarily

Doreen (*improvising*) No . . . I'm *in* tonight.
Dad Aren't you seeing whats-his-name?
Doreen Eric.
Dad That's him.
Doreen We never see each other on a Thursday. Anyway, tonight
I'm going to have my bath.
Dad You're sure he's not coming round to run your water for
you?
Doreen (*trying to laugh*) Oh Dad!
Dad (*turning to Doreen*) Straighten this there's a good girl.
Doreen (*straightening his tie*) Will you be back late tonight?

Dad About twelvish.

Doreen (*smiling*) Oh good.

Dad (*slightly suspicious*) What?

Doreen (*trying to cover up*) Well ... I'll be fast asleep by then so you won't wake me. (*She glances towards the sideboard*) Now what time is it?

Dad (*looking at his watch*) Twenty to eight.

Doreen What time are you supposed to be there?

Dad Half past.

Doreen Oh you've got plenty of time yet then.

Dad (*shouting*) Seven. It starts at half past seven.

Doreen turns Dad round and pushes him towards the stairs

Doreen Well you better hurry.

Dad (*ascending the stairs*) What the hell has happened to your mother?

Doreen (*suddenly remembering*) Oh ... it's Thursday.

Dad stops and looks at Doreen

Dad What?

Doreen Of course ... that's what's happened. She's gone to MacMurrys. You know, that little shop on the corner of West Street.

Dad (*he can't believe his ears*) That's half a mile away.

Doreen It's closed.

Dad (*shouting*) Closed?

Doreen All day on a Thursday.

Dad (*stepping back into the room*) Closed?

Doreen I don't know what she's going to do now.

Dad She'll have to go bare-legged that's all. Or wear trousers.

Doreen Pity it wasn't fancy dress or you could have done a swap. (*She is about to sit in the armchair*)

Dad (*stopping her*) Don't sit on that chair, Doreen, you'll crease your mother's coat.

There is a roll of thunder

Doreen We're in for a storm.

Dad Oh my God, did you hear that?

Doreen It's only thunder.

Dad Is it raining? (*He realizes he is missing a cuff-link*)

Doreen How should I know?

Dad goes to look in the dish on top of the television

Dad Have a look, will you?

Doreen exits to the front door

Doreen (*off*) I wouldn't be put off if it is. I mean you're going to take the car, aren't you?

Dad That's not what I'm worried about. (*He finds a cuff-link*)

Doreen (*off*) It's pouring.

Dad It's your mother, she's out in it.

Doreen enters

Doreen She's only wearing a dress. She'll catch her death.

Dad (*struggling to put in the cuff-link*) She'll catch more than that when I get hold of her.

Doreen It's a sudden storm. She didn't know it was going to rain. She only nipped out.

Dad (*panicking as he remembers*) What about her hair?

Doreen What about it?

Dad She paid eight pounds this morning to have it done.

Doreen Go and have a look for her in the car.

Dad It'll be ruined.

Doreen Perhaps she's hiding in a doorway.

Dad Well *you'd* better go and look for her then, because if she sees the look on *my* face she'll never come out.

Doreen She's probably as dry as a cork. She's not stupid . . . she's hiding somewhere.

Dad If she doesn't hurry up we'll miss the first course.

Doreen I wouldn't worry about the dinner if I were you.

Dad I can't see us getting there until after eight.

The front door slams

Mam enters. She stands, absolutely soaked through to the skin, her hair flat to her head from the rain. She has a pair of tights in one hand and a bunch of keys in the other

Dad Hell's delight!

Mam (*shouting*) Don't start on me.

Dad (*also shouting*) Look at you.

Mam (*shouting even louder*) I said, don't start on me.

Dad (*taking one small step towards her*) Where the hell have you been?

Mam Where do you think I've been? I went to get some tights.

Dad (*looking at his watch*) Do you know what time it is?

Mam (*to Doreen*) I'm soaked through.

Dad And look at your hair.

Mam (*to Dad*) It came on me all of a sudden.

Doreen You'll have to wear something else, Mam.

Mam I'll wear my green dress with the lurex sleeves.

Doreen Where is it?

Mam In the wardrobe.

Doreen makes for the stairs

What about my hair? (*She goes to look at it in the mirror*)

Dad (*taking another step towards her*) I'm glad you asked that.

Doreen I'll blow-dry it.

Doreen exits upstairs

Dad It's quarter to eight.

Mam All right, all right, don't fuss. Anyone would think we're going to meet royalty.

Dad (*with an air of expectancy*) You don't know who might be there.

Mam It's only the Pigeon Club's Annual Dinner.

Dad That's not the point. (*He paces in front of the settee*) Now hurry up.

Mam I *can't* do anything yet. What's the matter, are you afraid the corn is going to get cold?

Dad It starts at half past seven.

Mam You're not going to be *that* late.

Dad (*still pacing about*) Look at you. It takes you an hour to get ready under normal circumstances. You don't look as if you're going to be ready until twelve.

Mam Don't fuss.

Dad Fuss? What do you mean, fuss? I'm not fussing.

Mam Well sit down then.

Dad (*sitting*) What the hell made you go out at this time of night, anyway?

Mam (*going to him*) I told you ... a ladder about, (*she indicates with her fingers*) that big.

Dad You didn't even take an umbrella.

Mam I didn't know it was going to rain.

Dad This is a very important night for me.

Mam Well, there you are then. You couldn't see me go out with a ladder, could you? (*Slight pause*) And what do you mean, important?

Dad It is.

Mam You must be joking.

Dad I'm going to be presented with an award, aren't I?

Mam Some award. Fifth prize for pigeon breeding.

Dad (*a little hurt*) It's the first thing I've ever won.

Mam Anyone would think it was the Oscars.

Dad Well it is, in a way.

Mam Dai "Pidgeon" they call you, not Walter.

Dad (*shouting*) Are you going to hurry up?

Mam When are you going to get it into your head—I can't do anything yet.

Dad Well, start drying your hair or something.

Mam Fetch me a towel then.

Dad Where is it?

Mam Where it always is, hanging behind the back door.

Dad exits to the kitchen

Mam takes the dining-chair and, placing it between the table and the armchair, she sits on it

Dad (*off*) You should have made sure you had decent tights this afternoon.

Mam They were decent this afternoon. I laddered them putting them on.

Dad (*off*) Women, I don't know.

Mam I suppose you would have liked to see me go bare-legged.

Dad enters with a towel in his hand

Dad You could have ... it'll be dark ... no-one would know. (*He hands her the towel*)

Mam Well, do it for me then.

Dad puts the towel over Mam's head and begins to dry her hair

Dad I hope they're late serving the food.

Mam (*from under the towel*) There's a funny smell on this towel. Are you sure you got it from behind the door?

Dad Yes. Well . . . no. It had fallen. It was down by the side of the sink-unit.

Mam snatches the towel from her head and throws it across the room

Mam (*shouting*) That's the bloody floorcloth, what the hell's the matter with you.

Dad (*going after it and picking it up*) Well I didn't know.

Mam Oh you make me sick sometimes.

Dad sniffs the towel

> *Doreen enters carrying the green dress, a hair-dryer and a comb*

Doreen Right then, Mam, come and put this dress on.

Mam (*standing*) Don't you want to do my hair first?

Doreen I'll do it after.

Mam (*going to Doreen*) That dress is all right, isn't it?

Doreen Yes . . . it's lovely.

Mam (*to Dad*) Do you like it? (*She turns back to Doreen*) Show it to him.

Doreen holds up a revolting green dress

Dad (*swallowing hard; pause*) If I'd known you had the guts to wear that I'd have worn my mauve tie.

> *Mam exits to the kitchen, snatching the dress from Doreen as she goes*

Mam (*as she goes*) I should have known better than to ask.

> *Doreen exits to the kitchen leaving the hair-dryer and comb on the table*

Dad moves to the armchair

Dad (*to Mam*) You've got the tickets safe, haven't you? (*He puts his foot up on the arm of the chair and wipes his shoe with the floorcloth*)

Mam (*off*) I can't hear you.

Dad I said, you've got the tickets safe.

Mam (*off*) What tickets?

Dad For the dinner. (*He repeats the move with the other foot*)
Mam (*off*) I haven't seen any tickets.
Dad I gave them to you yesterday.
Mam (*off*) You didn't.

Dad moves to the kitchen doorway and throws the floorcloth in

Dad Don't tell me you've lost the tickets?
Mam (*off; shouting*) I haven't seen the tickets.
Dad I definitely remember giving them to you yesterday.

Mam enters from the kitchen wearing the green dress. She sits on the dining-chair

Doreen enters from the kitchen and plugs in the hair-dryer

Mam Have a look in my handbag.
Dad Where is it?
Mam I don't know. Behind the settee somewhere.
Dad (*disappearing behind the settee*) Time's getting on.
Mam And he says I nag.
Dad (*reappearing with a cream handbag*) There's nothing in this, it's empty.
Mam Not that one—my black one.
Dad (*disappearing behind the settee again*) How many bloody handbags have you got?
Mam Ten.
Dad (*reappearing suddenly*) Ten?
Mam I thought that would give you something to say.
Doreen Now sit still. (*She switches on the hair-dryer*)
Mam (*speaking over the noise*) Have a look *on* the settee.

Dad looks on the settee

Doreen I wonder what time it is now?
Mam What did you say?
Doreen I said, I wonder what time it is now.

Mam looks at her wrist and realizes she isn't wearing her watch

Mam I'm glad you asked that, I've forgotten to put my watch on.
Dad It's nearly five to. Is this it? (*He holds up a red handbag*)
Mam (*shouting*) Black I said, black. What's the matter, are you blind?

Dad I'm sure you've got more handbags than I've got socks. (*He finds another one*) What about this?

Mam That's it.

Doreen You'll have to hurry Mam, it's nearly five to.

Dad (*looking inside it*) I'll be lucky to find anything in this.

Mam Why?

Dad Look at it? Have you seen anything like it? (*He empties the contents of the bag one by one on to the settee*) A knife . . . a comb . . . an orange . . . a lipstick . . . a fork . . . an ashtray. An ashtray? A jelly. I don't believe this, a handbag . . . needle and cotton . . . a packet of biscuits . . . a tin of beans, and a mug.

Mam Did you find anything?

Dad (*refilling the handbag*) They're not there.

Mam I can't hear you.

Dad (*louder*) I said they're not there.

Mam Turn it off a minute, Doreen.

Doreen turns off the hair-dryer

What did you say?

Dad I said, they're not there.

Mam Well I told you I didn't have them, didn't I?

Dad You must have put them somewhere else.

Mam (*becoming annoyed*) You won't listen to me, will you?

Doreen If I don't get on, Mam, you'll never get there.

Dad, having eventually refilled the handbag, drops it behind the settee and goes over to the sideboard to look for the tickets there

Dad If she doesn't find those tickets we can't go anyway.

Mam That's right, blame me.

Doreen Look, can I carry on?

Mam Depends who he is.

Doreen I mean with your hair.

Doreen continues drying her mother's hair

Dad I hope you haven't thrown them out.

Mam I can't hear you.

Dad takes a five pound note from his pocket

Dad Here you are, you'd better have this fiver in case you run short.

Mam (*immediately taking it from him*) Oh thank you very much, I could do with it.

Dad (*immediately taking it back*) I thought you'd hear that.

Mam We can get in without tickets, can't we?

Dad (*loudly*) No. It says on the bottom, "No tickets, no admittance".

Mam I'm sure you didn't give them to me.

Dad Would they be anywhere else?

Mam Speak up.

Dad (*louder*) Would they be anywhere else?

Mam You can have a look in the bedroom.

Dad In the where?

Mam On the dressing-table.

Dad Upstairs?

Mam I don't think they're there, though.

Dad (*ascending the stairs*) I should never have given them to you.

Mam What's that?

Dad Nothing.

Dad exits up the stairs

Doreen sighs heavily as she struggles with her mother's hair

Doreen It's not going right, Mam.

Mam What?

Doreen (*switching off the hair-dryer*) It's not right.

Mam What's not.

Doreen Your hair.

Mam What's the matter with it?

Doreen It's a mess.

Mam Roll it then.

Doreen You haven't got time.

Mam (*going to the mirror*) Well do something with it.

Doreen I think you'll have to wear your wig.

Mam (*turning to Doreen*) Oh no, I can't.

Doreen Why not?

Mam Because I haven't shown your father that I've bought it yet.

Doreen There's nothing else you can do, your own hair's like a rat's back.

Mam He'll go off his head when he sees it, I know he will.

Doreen No he won't. Where is it?

Mam In the box behind the settee.

Doreen (*disappearing behind the settee*) What's it like anyway, you haven't shown it to me yet. (*During Mam's next line, she throws several handbags, shoes, a catalogue etc. from behind the settee*)

Mam Well it's all right. No, it's nice. Well it ought to be, it cost me enough. I'll tell him it was in a sale. Six pounds in a sale, right, if he should ask. And sure as hell he will.

Doreen (*appearing holding a box*) Is this it?

Mam (*taking a small step nearer*) I'm not sure I should wear it tonight.

Doreen You haven't got a choice. (*Still standing behind the settee she puts the box down on the seat cushion to open it. There is a slight pause as she stares at it; amazed*) It's blonde.

Mam Yes. Thought I'd have a change.

Doreen (*taking it out*) What made you buy this?

Mam (*taking another small step nearer*) I was depressed. Your father doesn't take much notice of me these days so I thought, go on, have a blonde one.

Doreen You can't wear this to the pigeon dinner.

Mam I thought you said I didn't have a choice.

Doreen Well, you haven't. Not really.

Mam (*sitting on the settee*) That's it then, I won't go.

Doreen, slightly panic-stricken sits beside her mother on the settee

Doreen Oh yes . . . you must . . . you've got to.

Mam Why?

Doreen Because . . . well, it's Dad's big night, isn't it? And you can't disappoint him on his big night.

Mam I don't see why not, he disappointed me on mine.

Doreen You've got to go Mam. I won't have you let him down. Let's try it on.

Doreen rises and moves behind the settee in order to put the wig on her mother

Mam I don't know. I think if I stood one leg on a perch your father would take more notice of me.

Doreen (*adjusting it*) Now . . . let's see what it looks like.

Mam Fetch me a mirror.

Doreen Wait a minute, let me comb it first.

Doreen combs the wig

Mam It looked lovely on the model in the shop window.
Doreen It wouldn't be so bad if it wasn't blonde.
Mam Don't you think it'll make me look younger?
Doreen No.
Mam Well, it made the model look younger.
Doreen I dare say it would make *you* look younger if you were bald.
Mam What do you mean?
Doreen Like the model in the shop.
Mam She wasn't bald, she had a wig on.
Doreen Oh never mind.
Mam Get me a mirror.

Doreen looks and finds one on the sideboard

Doreen It looks better than I thought. (*She hands the mirror to Mam*)
Mam (*looking at it*) It doesn't look right to me.
Doreen Yes ... it's lovely. Come on, hurry up, or it won't be worth you going.
Mam It didn't look like this on the model.
Doreen No, I don't suppose it did.
Mam What's this bit here? (*She tugs at a piece of hair on her forehead*)
Doreen (*combing the piece of hair*) It's all right, Mam. Honest.

Mam looks at the wig from various angles in the mirror

Mam You've got it on back to front.
Doreen Don't be silly.
Mam Yes you have. I shouldn't have all this hair round the back of my neck.
Doreen (*looking at it*) Are you sure?
Mam The model in the shop didn't have a crop.
Doreen Let's try it then. (*She takes off the wig and puts it on the other way*) How's that?
Mam (*looking in the mirror again*) Well it feels better anyway. Yes, that's definitely the right way. (*Slight pause*) I think it looked better back to front though, don't you?
Doreen Leave it as it is ... it's all right.

Mam Does blonde suit me?

Doreen moves closer to get a better view

Doreen (*after a moment*) Oh no.
Mam I think it's nice.
Doreen You look as if you've got a ferret on your head.
Mam (*positively*) Oh well that's it then, I'm not going.

Doreen sits left of her mother on the settee masking her from anyone entering the room

Doreen No, I don't mean it. You look lovely. Honest you do.

Dad enters

Dad Well they're nowhere up there. I don't know what you've . . . (*He looks around the room but cannot see Mam*) Well where the hell is she now?
Doreen Who?
Dad Your mother.
Mam (*leaning forward*) I'm here.

Dad looks at her and does a double take

Dad (*slight pause*) Is that you?
Mam Of course it's me. (*Rather pleased with herself*) Who did you think it was?
Dad What's that ferret you've got on your head?
Mam It was six pounds in a sale.

Dad goes to the television and looks for the tickets there

Dad A jumble sale, was it?
Mam Very funny.
Dad They're not on the dressing-table.
Mam What do they look like?
Dad What do you mean, what do they look like?
Mam What colour are they?
Dad White.
Mam About that big? (*Indicating with her fingers*)
Dad Yes.
Mam With red printing?
Dad That's right.
Mam (*shaking her head*) No, I haven't seen them.

Dad I can't think where they can be.

Mam Have you looked on the sideboard?

Dad Have you *seen* the sideboard?

Mam I tidied it all this morning.

Dad You could lose the television on there and never find it.

Mam I'm fed up of putting things away after you.

Dad (*moving to the sideboard*) I went looking for my battery charger on there yesterday. It *is* there, I know it is. I'll just have to wait a couple of weeks for it to surface.

Mam So you didn't find it after all?

Dad No. But do you know what I did find? A ration book. You've got bills on there dating back before we went metric.

Mam It's all right ... don't worry, they've all been paid.

Doreen Don't you think you'd better go?

Dad They won't let us in without tickets.

Mam You can say what you like, you never gave them to me.

Doreen (*looking at the clock*) It's getting late.

Dad (*moving towards the kitchen doorway*) Where the hell shall we look for them?

Doreen They know you down there, Dad. They know you've bought tickets.

Dad (*to Mam*) Think now, will you? Think where you've put them.

Dad goes to the sideboard and opens the cupboard. As he does this all the contents rush out

Mam (*losing her temper*) Why won't you believe me when I tell you, I haven't seen them.

Dad (*piling the rubbish back in*) I remember giving them to you.

Mam I remember you saying you had them. I even remember you showing them to me. But I don't remember anything about you giving them to me to keep safe.

Doreen (*rising*) Let's all have a look together.

Dad looks around the room almost exhausted

Dad They've got to be here somewhere.

Mam goes to the table and gets down on all fours

Mam Perhaps they've fallen down under the table.

Dad Have a look on the sideboard, Doreen. You've got more time than I have.

Doreen looks on the sideboard

I'll look in the kitchen. I wouldn't mind betting she's put them in the fridge.

Dad exits to the kitchen

Mam (*from under the table*) It's pointless looking on the sideboard, Doreen. Have a look behind the settee.

Doreen goes to look behind the settee and disappears from sight

I've half a mind not to go.

Eric enters the hall

Eric (*quietly*) Hello?

Mam backs out slightly from under the table. Eric sees her backside

Doreen He's been waiting for this for weeks.

Eric cannot believe his ears

He mustn't be disappointed now.

Eric crosses and caresses Mam's backside

Eric I won't be I promise.

Pause; Mam's head appears from under the tablecloth. She is facing centre stage

Mam Are you sure you wouldn't rather a night in?
Eric (*still holding her backside*) Who's this?
Doreen (*unseen*) Eric?

Eric lets go of Mam's backside and steps back

Dad (*off*) Have you found them?

Doreen pops up from behind the settee

Doreen What's going on?

Eric turns to face Doreen and points to Mam's backside

Eric I thought she was. . . . What are you doing down there?

Doreen Looking for tickets.
Mam (*in the same position*) We could stay in if you wanted to.

Dad enters from the kitchen

Dad What did you say? (*To Eric*) What are you doing here?
Eric (*backing away*) Oh ... hello.

Mam comes out from under the table and bangs her head

Mam Who's that? (*She goes and stands next to Dad*)
Eric (*to Mam and Dad*) I thought you were going out.
Dad (*to Doreen*) I thought you were having a bath.
Doreen (*to Eric*) I thought I wasn't seeing you tonight.
Mam (*slipping her arm round Dad*) I thought perhaps we'd go to bed early.
Dad (*stepping away from her*) What the hell are you going on about? (*Shouting*) And straighten that wig.

Mam straightens the wig

Eric (*recognizing her*) Oh ... it's you.
Mam Who did you think it was?
Eric (*pointing to Doreen*) Her.
Doreen (*insulted*) I don't look like that.
Dad Did anyone find anything?
Mam }
Doreen } (*together*) No.
Eric What are you looking for?
Dad Our dinner and dance tickets.
Eric The white ones?
Dad Yes.
Eric With red printing?
Dad That's right.
Eric Don't you know where they are?
Dad Have you seen them?
Eric (*shaking his head*) Sorry.
Mam (*ascending the stairs*) I expect they're in the bedroom. I bet they're right in front of your eyes somewhere.

Mam exits upstairs

Dad (*shouting after her*) They wouldn't be in the bathroom I suppose?

Doreen comes from behind the settee and stands in front of it

Doreen (*to Dad*) Why don't you have a look.
Dad (*ascending the stairs*) I'll kill her if they are.

Dad exits upstairs

Eric and Doreen take a long desirable look at each other

Doreen (*stepping towards him*) Lollipop!
Eric Dumpling!

Eric and Doreen embrace each other

I thought they would have gone by now.
Doreen We've had problems.

Eric grabs Doreen and pushes her down on the settee. He sits beside her

Eric I must have you.
Doreen Patience.
Eric Your body is ... is ... doing things to me.
Doreen Calm down ... You're beginning to stutter.

Eric pulls Doreen on to his lap

Eric My feet didn't touch the ground all the way over here.

Doreen fights to regain her previous position

Doreen You only live next door.
Eric If I don't have you soon I'll ex ... ex ... explode.
Doreen If they don't find those tickets they're not going to go out.
Eric They'll have to.

Eric again tries to pull Doreen on to his lap

I can't ... can't ... can't wait a minute longer for you.

Dad is heard shouting from the top of the stairs

It's your father, he ... he ... he's coming back.
Doreen Sit and act natural.
Eric How do I ... do I ... do I do that?
Doreen Stay calm and don't stutter then he won't suspect. And cross your legs.

Doreen and Eric both cross their legs simultaneously

> *Dad enters down the stairs taking his jacket from the banister at the bottom of the stairs as he comes. He puts it on*

Dad It's a waste of time; they'd never be up there.

Doreen Perhaps Mam will find them now in the bedroom.

Dad She'll be lucky.

Eric Why down you sit . . . sit . . . sit down. I'm sure they'll turn up somewhere.

Dad Why are you stuttering?

Eric I'm . . . I'm . . . I'm not. I'm . . . I'm trying to keep calm.

Dad What have *you* got to be excited about?

Eric Noth . . . noth . . . noth——

Dad Nothing.

Eric That's right.

Dad What do you want anyway?

Eric Wa . . . wa . . . want?

Dad You don't see Doreen on a Thursday.

Doreen (*improvising*) He came to make a phone call. (*To Eric*) Didn't you?

Eric nods

Dad What's the matter with his own phone?

Doreen He's been cut off. There's something wrong with it.

Dad stands and waits for Eric to use the telephone. Eric continues to sit on the settee with Doreen

Dad (*shouting*) Well get on with it then . . . And don't forget to put your money in the box.

Eric springs to his feet

There is a blood curdling scream from upstairs

Eric (*panic-stricken*) Who . . .

Doreen (*standing; shouting*) Mam?

Eric Who . . . who . . .

Dad (*to Doreen*) What's happened?

Eric Who . . . who . . .

Dad and Doreen run to the bottom of the stairs

Doreen (*calling up the stairs*) Are you all right?
Eric Who . . .
Dad (*calling*) What's going on?
Eric Who . . . who . . .
Mam (*off*) I'm all right.
Eric Who . . .
Dad What did she scream for?
Doreen She's coming down.
Eric Who . . .

Mam enters down the stairs

Mam Here I am.
Eric Who . . .
Dad What happened?
Doreen Why did you scream?
Eric . . . was that? (*He is out of breath and relieved that he has at last got it out*)
Mam (*visibly shaken*) It was my own fault. I was taken by surprise.

Doreen and Dad take Mum by the arms and lead her to the armchair

Doreen (*sitting her down*) You frightened us.
Mam I frightened myself. I forgot I had this wig on. I caught sight of myself in the wardrobe mirror and I almost died.
Dad Did you find them?
Mam What?
Dad (*shouting*) The bloody tickets.
Mam No I didn't.
Dad (*turning away*) Well that's it then. It's all off.
Doreen They've got to be around here somewhere.
Eric Why . . . why . . . don't——
Dad (*looking on the sideboard*) I wouldn't be surprised if they've been thrown in the fire.
Eric Why . . . don't——
Mam Now who would throw them in the fire?
Eric Why——
Dad You.
Mam Oh don't talk soft.
Eric Why don't——
Dad (*shouting over his shoulder to Mam*) Seven pounds they cost me.

Eric Why don't you look——
Dad They *must* be here somewhere.
Eric Why don't you have a look in your pocket?
Dad Don't be silly, they wouldn't be in there.
Mam (*demandingly*) Have a look.
Dad (*putting his right hand in his left inside pocket*) I'm telling you, they wouldn't be there. (*He puts his left hand in his right inside pocket*) I've already looked through this coat once. (*He taps both side pockets with the palms of his hands. As he speaks he takes out the tickets; slight pause*) Who the hell put those in there?
Mam I told you I didn't have them.
Dad And I'm damn sure I didn't.
Doreen It doesn't matter who did, you've got them now, so go.
Mam (*looking at her feet*) I can't go yet, I haven't changed my shoes.
Dad (*raising his voice*) You've been getting ready since six o'clock and you still haven't changed your shoes.
Mam I've been busy looking for those tickets.
Dad I'm going to start the car. Be ready in two minutes. (*He turns to leave*)
Mam You'd better give those tickets to me or they'll go missing again.
Dad They're all right here.

Dad puts the tickets into a vase on the sideboard so that they are just sticking out of the top. He then takes his raincoat from the banister and puts it on

Dad exits

Mam (*taking off her shoes*) Now then, my shoes.
Doreen I'll get them. Where are they?
Mam Under the sideboard I expect.
Doreen (*looking for them*) Which ones are you going to wear?
Mam The green ones.
Doreen (*handing them to her*) Here you are.
Mam (*looking at the ladder in her tights*) Hell, I still haven't changed my tights.
Doreen Well hurry up for goodness sake.

Mam leaves her old shoes on the floor. She takes her tights and the green shoes from Doreen and heads for the stairs

Mam If your father toots, tell him I won't be long. Tell him I'm on the toilet or something.

Mam exits upstairs

Eric sits on the settee. Doreen looks at Eric, who crosses and uncrosses his legs

Doreen (*half apologetic, half excited*) Won't be long now.

Eric I'm bursting at the seams.

Doreen (*moving to the armchair*) Well don't burst yet or they'll twig it.

Eric Come and sit next to me.

Doreen I'd better not. You'll only get excited and start stuttering again.

Eric Well, don't stand where I can see your . . . your body, it's doing things to me.

Doreen (*flattered*) Where would you like me to stand then, in the kitchen? (*She giggles*)

Eric Just sit down, I'll be all right then.

Doreen sits in the armchair

Doreen You seem to be extra passionate tonight.

Eric I've worked myself up. I've been waiting for this for days.

Doreen A girl can't rush these things.

Eric Oh I'm not complaining. I've just got myself into a bit of a state, that's all.

Doreen Well, never mind, five more minutes and they'll be gone.

Eric (*excitedly*) Yes.

Doreen (*a slight pause*) You do love me, lollipop, don't you?

Eric Of course I do.

Doreen I mean, you don't only want me for my body.

Eric (*shaking his head*) No.

Doreen There are other things as well.

Eric (*nodding his head*) Yes.

Doreen Like what?

Eric (*a slight pause*) Well . . . like, you know . . . like . . . sex.

Doreen You didn't understand. Do you love me for other things.

Eric (*confidently*) Oh yes.

Doreen Tell me what they are then.

Eric (*a slight pause*) I don't know what you mean Do——

Doreen Well, like my personality. (*She goes to him*) My conversation, and things like that.

Eric Oh yeah, I like all those.

Doreen So it's not just a physical thing?

Eric No.

Doreen I'm glad.

Eric uncrosses and crosses his legs

You don't look very comfortable like that.

Eric I'm not.

Doreen Well you don't have to keep your legs crossed when there's no-one here.

Eric uncrosses and crosses his legs

Eric (*with relief*) Oh that's better.

Doreen Your trousers are too small for you I expect.

Eric No, they fitted me all right in *my* house.

Doreen turns away from Eric

Doreen (*slight pause*) You did mean what you said, didn't you?

Eric About what?

Doreen You know. (*She turns to face him*) Yesterday. The engagement ring.

Eric (*panicking slightly*) Yes, but a man ... man ... man can't rush these things.

Doreen No I know. I just put my mind on it, that's all.

Eric (*swallowing hard*) Have you? It's a big step.

Doreen puts her right knee on the arm of the settee and leans over Eric

Doreen I know about big steps. There are thirteen of them to my bedroom. (*She glances first over to the stairs, and then back to Eric. Their faces are inches apart*) I thought we could go on Saturday.

Eric I'd ... I'd ... I'd have to save.

Doreen runs around the back of the settee and sits beside Eric

Doreen We could have a nice day out shopping.

Eric I haven't saved enough.

Doreen I have, I'll lend you the money.

Eric Well I——

Doreen You won't have to give it back to me straight away.

Eric I'd rather wait.

Doreen And we'll keep it our little secret. We won't tell anyone.

Eric (*realizing he's beaten*) I don't think I've got much choice, have I?

Doreen Not if you're still bursting at the seams.

Eric (*pause; reluctantly*) What time shall I call for you on Saturday?

Doreen We'll decide later. Oh I'm so excited.

Eric You're sure you won't tell anybody?

Doreen Not if you don't want me to.

Eric I'd rather keep it quiet.

Doreen I won't tell a soul. I won't even put it on my finger, I'll wear it round my neck.

Eric Good. The less people that know about it the better.

Doreen Why?

Eric They'd only say we're rushing it. I mean we've only been going out a fortnight.

Doreen Is that all? It seems as if I've known you all my life.

Eric You have.

Doreen (*still excited*) Oh I feel like giving you a big kiss ...

Their heads zoom towards each other but Doreen turns away at the last minute

... but I better wait till later.

Eric How much longer are they going to be?

Doreen Any minute now.

Eric I'm beginning to have the shakes.

Doreen Would it be better if *I* crossed *my* legs?

Eric (*panicking*) There's your mother.

They both cross their legs and sit bolt upright

Mam enters down the stairs

Mam It's marvellous, isn't it? After all *his* shouting it's *me* who's waiting for *him*. How do I look?

Doreen Lovely.

Mam (*adjusting the rows of beads around her neck*) Are you sure? I feel a bit over-dressed.

Doreen No, you're all right.

Mam Where's my coat?

Doreen (*looking around the room*) On the back of the chair.

Mam I'd better put it on, it's still raining. (*She puts on her coat*) Anyone seen my handbag?

Doreen Which one?

Mam It had better be the green one. What do you think?

Doreen Yes, I think so.

Mam (*looking around the room*) I've seen it about here somewhere.

Doreen (*pointing to it*) There it is on the telly.

Mam Oh yes. (*She takes it and opens it. As she peers in, her head is knocked back with the odour which is exuding from the bag*) Oh, good God!

Doreen What's the matter?

Mam I'd forgotten about these. (*She ventures in with her thumb and index finger and takes out a small packet of something*) It's half a bag of cockles. I bought them in the club a fortnight ago. (*She holds them, arm outstretched, towards Doreen*) Put them in the bin, will you, Doreen?

Doreen takes them from her mother and exits to the kitchen

Now then, air freshener. (*She takes a tin of air freshener from the top of the television and sprays the inside of the bag. She smells inside*) That's better. (*She puts the air freshener back on the television*) Only my purse now.

Doreen enters from the kitchen and, taking Mam's purse from the sideboard, gives it to her

Doreen Here you are

Mam Lovely. (*She puts it in her handbag*) Well, that's me done. I'm ready. (*Pause*) I wonder what's keeping your father?

Doreen You may as well sit down till he comes.

Doreen sits next to Eric on the settee and Mam sits in the armchair

Mam You're sure he hasn't tooted?

Doreen We haven't heard anything. (*To Eric*) Have we?

Eric No ... nothing.

Mam What's the time?

Doreen (*looking at the clock*) Just gone ten past.
Mam Should be there for the apple tart and custard then.
Doreen You're not *that* late.

Doreen and Eric uncross and cross their legs simultaneously. There is a pause. Mam tugs at the back of her wig, then brushes the front of her coat down with her hand. She looks at her shoes to check they are suitable

Mam You're *sure* I look all right?
Doreen Yes.
Mam I don't feel comfortable. It must be the wig.
Doreen There's nothing wrong with the wig.
Mam I didn't say there was anything wrong with it. I just said it wasn't comfortable.

The front door slams

Dad enters. He is very wet

Dad I can't start the bloody car.
Mam Well, why's that?
Dad (*taking off his raincoat; shouting*) Because the battery's flat, that's why. (*He hangs his coat on the banister*)
Mam I thought you charged it yesterday.
Dad I was going to but I couldn't find the charger.
Mam It's on the sideboard somewhere.
Dad (*exasperated*) That's why I couldn't find it.
Mam What are we going to do now?
Dad (*turning his back on her*) I don't know.
Mam We'll just have to stay home then, that's all.

Dad	(*turning to face her*) You'd like that wouldn't you? I knew you weren't fussy to go in the first place.
Doreen (*together*)	Well there's no need to do that. You'll have to go now, everything's been arranged.
Eric	What's the point of staying home? There must be some other way of getting there.

Mam (*standing*) Hold it . . . hold it, wait, wait a minute, what's the matter with you all?

Dad (*taking one step nearer to Mam*) Well it's all right for you. Tonight's my big night. Tonight I'm getting an award.

Mam (*taking a step nearer Dad*) Award? Award? A plastic pigeon on a wooden stand.

Dad That's not the point.

Eric Why don't you ring for a taxi?

Doreen Of course.

Dad (*to Mam*) Why didn't I think of that?

Mam Because it takes brains.

Dad (*nodding to Eric*) Why did he think of it then. (*He goes to the telephone*) Have you got a number?

Mam I think there's one on the calendar. (*She goes to look at the calendar; shouting*) Three-two-one-three-one.

Dad (*dialing*) Three-one-two——

Mam (*shouting*) Three-two-one.

Dad (*replacing the receiver and dialing again*) Three–two–one——

Mam Three-one.

Dad I know. Three-one. (*He speaks into the receiver with an attempted distinguished voice*) Hello? ... This is Mister Thomas speaking. I wonder if I might book a taxi for this evening? ... Er ... Nine Decimal Row. ... To the Working Men's Club. ... Yes. ... Oh jolly good ...

Mam and Doreen look at each other

Well, as soon as possible ... (*Beginning to lose his accent*) What do you mean, you can't? ... What do you mean you can't fit us in until nine? ...

Eric groans. He and Doreen uncross and cross their legs

But I want one now. ... (*He tries to control himself and maintain his accent*) I mean, I need one immediately, I'm late for the awards you see. ... Yes, I'm being presented. ...

Mam tuts

Could you possibly? I'd be most grateful. ... Thank you. (*He replaces the receiver and speaks in his own voice*) There'll be one round in five minutes.

Mam (*in a very refined accent*) It's amazin' wot a little charm and refinement can do, in it?

Dad You are ready, I suppose?

Mam As ready as I'll ever be.

Dad I hope they're not serving chicken tonight.

Eric leans forward to do up his shoe lace

Mam Why?

Dad (*pointing to the wig*) Because that ferret will have a feast if they do.

Mam (*a little upset*) Oh don't make fun. You always make fun. You never say anything nice.

Dad Well look at it. I don't know what you think you look like.

Mam (*hurt*) I only bought it for you.

Dad It would look better on me too.

Mam Well wear the bloody thing then. (*She snatches it from her head and throws it at him, but she misses and it hits Eric*)

Doreen (*reaching for the wig*) Oh Mam!

Mam I'm fed up with him.

Dad I didn't mean it.

Mam Why make fun then?

Dad I'm all worked up, that's all.

Eric I know how you feel.

Dad I expect I'm a bit nervous.

Doreen (*going to Mam*) Come on Mam. It looks lovely, honest.

Mam (*to Dad*) Does it?

Doreen holds up the wig

Dad (*swallowing hard*) Yes.

Mam goes and sits on the dining-chair

Mam (to Doreen) Put it back on then.

Doreen puts the wig back on to Mam's head

(*To Dad*) But I'm warning you, one word from you tonight and I'll tell everyone about your operation.

Dad (*sitting in the armchair*) You wouldn't

Mam Just try me.

Doreen Come on now, don't quarrel. You're going to have a nice night out together.

There is a slight pause

Mam Five minutes you said that taxi would be?

Dad That's what they said.

Mam Shouldn't be long then.

Doreen (*having finished replacing Mam's wig*) There you are, as good as new.

Mam Are you sure?

Doreen Do you want a mirror?

Mam No, go on, I'll trust you.

Doreen Yes, it's looking nice, Mam. You'll have to wear it to my engagement par ... ty. (*She pretends it has slipped out*)

Eric looks at her

Dad (*standing*) Your what?

Doreen Er ... my engagement, I mean our engagement party.

Dad You two are not getting engaged?

Doreen ⎫ (*together*)   Yes.

Eric ⎭   No. (*To Doreen*) I thought it was a secret?

Doreen It slipped out.

Eric I'll remember that later.

Mam Oh, I think I'm going to cry.

Dad (*turning towards Mam*) Oh shut up.

Doreen (*sitting down next to Eric*) Are you pleased Mam?

Dad (*to Doreen*) You haven't been going out together five minutes.

Doreen We've known each other all our lives. Grown up together. Played ... house and ... things, together.

Eric (*to Doreen*) No-one was supposed to know.

Mam Have you named the day?

Doreen No, but we're buying the ring on Saturday.

Dad (*sitting in the armchair*) Well ... what can I say?

Mam You're not speechless?

Eric I am.

Mam (*standing*) I've got an idea. Why don't we forget about this pigeon dinner and the four of us go out for a celebration drink?

Doreen ⎫   Well there's no need to do that. We can have a celebration again.

Dad ⎬ (*together*) What do you mean forget about the dinner? And I've ordered the taxi now as well.

Eric ⎭   I wouldn't bother if I were you. We can always have a drink another time

Mam (*shouting*) All right forget about it, forget about it. It was only a thought.

Dad Anything to get out of it.

Mam (*sitting*) It's not every day your daughter gets engaged.

Eric She's not.

They all look at Eric

   Well, not yet anyway.

Mam I only suggested it because I thought it would be a nice night out.

Dad You'll have a nice night out now at the dinner.

Mam No-one has a nice night out at them dinners. Well . . . only the pigeons perhaps.

Dad There's not going to be any pigeons there *tonight*.

Mam There were last year.

Dad Yes, but that was a mistake. Anyway they won't have any there this year because they've changed the caterer.

A car horn sounds

   That's the taxi. (*He stands*)

Mam (*standing*) Are you ready?

Dad I've been ready for over an hour.

Mam Well come on then, let's go.

Doreen Have a nice time.

Mam and Dad move into the hallway

Mam (*to Dad*) You should have your mac, it's still raining.

Dad (*grabbing his coat from the banister*) Don't *you* tell *me* about getting wet.

Mam (*to Dad; shouting*) Oh shut up. (*Sweetly to Doreen and Eric*) So long then.

Doreen goes to see Mam and Dad off

   Mam and Dad exit

Doreen See you later.

The front door slams

Doreen (*turning back into the room*) At last.

Eric looks away from her

What's the matter?

He doesn't answer

You're not going to pout are you?

Eric (*pouting*) I thought it was going to be a secret.

Doreen It's only my mother and father. They won't tell anybody.

Eric Are you kidding? By nine o'clock tonight it'll be all round the Pigeon Club.

Doreen Come and give me a kiss.

Eric crosses to Doreen and embraces her

   Mam rushes in

Eric and Doreen spring apart

Mam We've gone and forgotten these now. (*She takes the tickets from the vase*) So long.

   Mam exits

Doreen and Eric embrace again

Doreen (*still in his arms*) Well . . . that's it. We're all by ourselves.

Eric I thought they'd never go. (*He kisses her*)

Doreen It's still there then?

Eric What?

Doreen The passion.

Eric Oh yes.

They look into each others eyes for a moment

Doreen What do you want to do now?

Eric That's a silly question. (*He eases her towards the stairs*)

Doreen Don't you think it's a bit soon?

Eric Well, we have been going out a fortnight.

Doreen I mean too soon after they've left.

Eric They're not likely to come back, are they?

Doreen I shouldn't think so, but you never know.

Eric I . . . I . . . think I'll take the chance.

Doreen You're stuttering again.

Eric That's because I'm ex . . . ex . . . ex——

Doreen Excited.

Eric Yes.

Doreen Does it always affect you like that?
Eric Ye . . . ye . . . ye——
Doreen Oh never mind, we haven't got all night.
Eric Let's go . . . let's . . . let's . . . let's go up then.

Doreen ascends the stairs pulling Eric up behind her

Doreen You'll like my bedroom, it's got lovely wallpaper.
Eric To . . . to . . . to hell with the wallpaper.

Suddenly voices are heard outside

Dad (*off*) Well, it's not my fault.
Mam (*off*) Who the hell's fault is it then?

Doreen and Eric are frozen on the stairs

Eric Oh my . . .
Doreen They're back. They've come back.
Eric My . . .

Mam enters in a fury, followed by Dad

Mam You should have looked at the tickets. (*She collapses in the armchair*)
Eric My . . .
Dad I did.
Eric (*squeezing it out*) God!
Doreen (*still on the stairs*) What's the matter?
Mam Oh, he got the dates wrong, didn't he? The bloody dinner's not till next week.
Dad (*to Doreen*) Where are you off to?
Doreen (*improvising*) I'm going to have my bath.
Dad (*to Eric*) And where do you think you're going to?
Eric (*panicking*) M . . . m . . . m . . . me? Oh I'm . . . I'm . . . I'm just going to wash her back.

Black-out

CURTAIN

FURNITURE AND PROPERTY LIST

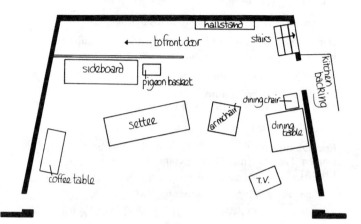

On the diagram: hallstand, stairs, ← to front door, sideboard, pigeon basket, kitchen backing, dining chair, armchair, settee, dining table, coffee table, T.V.

On stage: Dining-table. *On it:* dirty dishes, box of groceries, remains of a Chinese meal. *Under it:* shoes

Dining-chair

Armchair. *On it:* fur coat

Settee. *On it:* cushions, magazines, a red handbag, a black handbag. *In the black handbag:* a knife, comb, lipstick, fork, an orange, an ashtray, a jelly, another handbag, needle and cotton, a packet of biscuits, tin of beans, a mug.

Behind settee: cream handbag, shoes, catalogue, box with blonde wig in

Sideboard. *On it:* general clutter including a clock, vase, telephone, purse, a mirror. *In its cupboards:* assorted rubbish. *Under it:* a pair of green shoes

Television. *On it:* can of air freshener, dish containing cuff-link, green handbag. *In the green handbag:* half a bag of cockles

Coffee-table. *On it:* record player, records

Hall stand. *On it:* coats, umbrellas

Stairs with banister. *On the bottom of banister:* raincoat, jacket with 2 tickets in the pocket

Mirror. *Behind it:* letters, bills

Calendar

Pigeon basket

Electric socket (practical)

Off stage: Mauve tie **(Dad)**
              Blue tie **(Dad)**
              Pair of tights **(Mam)**
              Bunch of keys **(Mam)**
              Floorcloth **(Dad)**
              Green dress **(Doreen)**
              Hair-dryer **(Doreen)**
              Comb **(Doreen)**
              Rows of beads **(Mam)**

Personal: **Dad:** watch
              Dad: cuff link
              Dad: five pound note

LIGHTING PLOT

To open: General lighting

Cue 1   "I'm just going to wash her back."   (Page 31)
           Black-out

EFFECTS PLOT

MADE AND PRINTED IN GREAT BRITAIN BY
· LATIMER TREND & COMPANY LTD PLYMOUTH
MADE IN ENGLAND